Buddy the Brain

Written and Illustrated by Alison Rheaume, MS

Paperback ISBN 979-8-9938918-1-1

Library of Congress Control Number: 2025926831
City of Publication: Franklin, MA / Printed in the USA
First edition printing, February 2026, by Embracing Unique

Cover design, illustrations, and typography by Alison Rheaume
Edited by Tisha Martin

https://alirheaume.com

This book is dedicated to:
Emery, Leo, and Eli

Auntie Ali loves you!

Hi, I am Buddy the Brain!

I live inside your head.

You may think I am invisible because you cannot see me,

but I am in your head and
I help you do cool things.

Can you take a deep
breath in and out?

Buddy the Brain
helped you do that.

Can you wiggle your body?

Buddy the Brain
helped you do that.

Can you laugh?

Buddy the Brain
helped you do that.

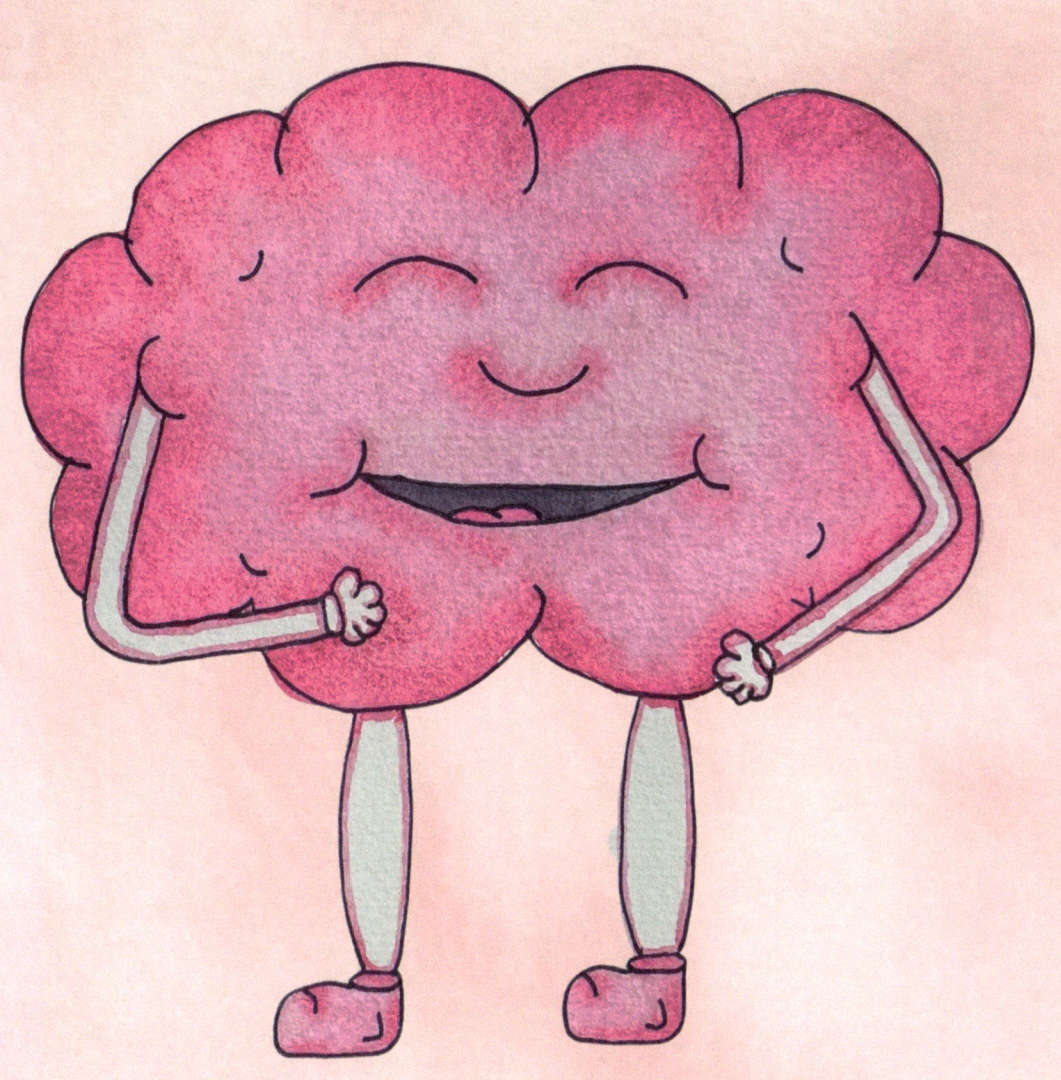

What else do you
think Buddy the Brain

can help you do?

It is important to keep
Buddy the Brain Safe,

so he can keep helping you grow, learn, and have fun!

You can keep Buddy
the Brain safe by...

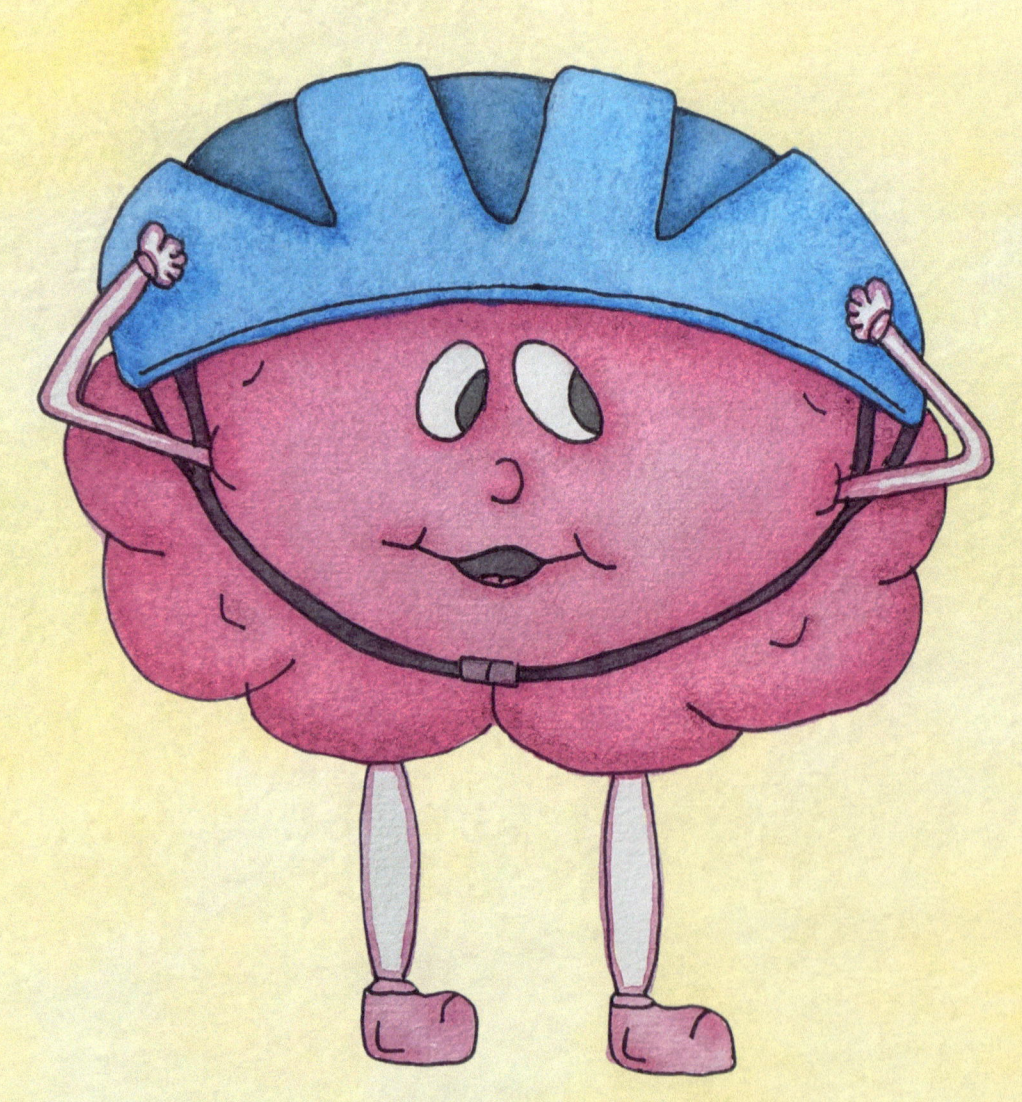

wearing a helmet.

You can keep Buddy
the Brain safe by...

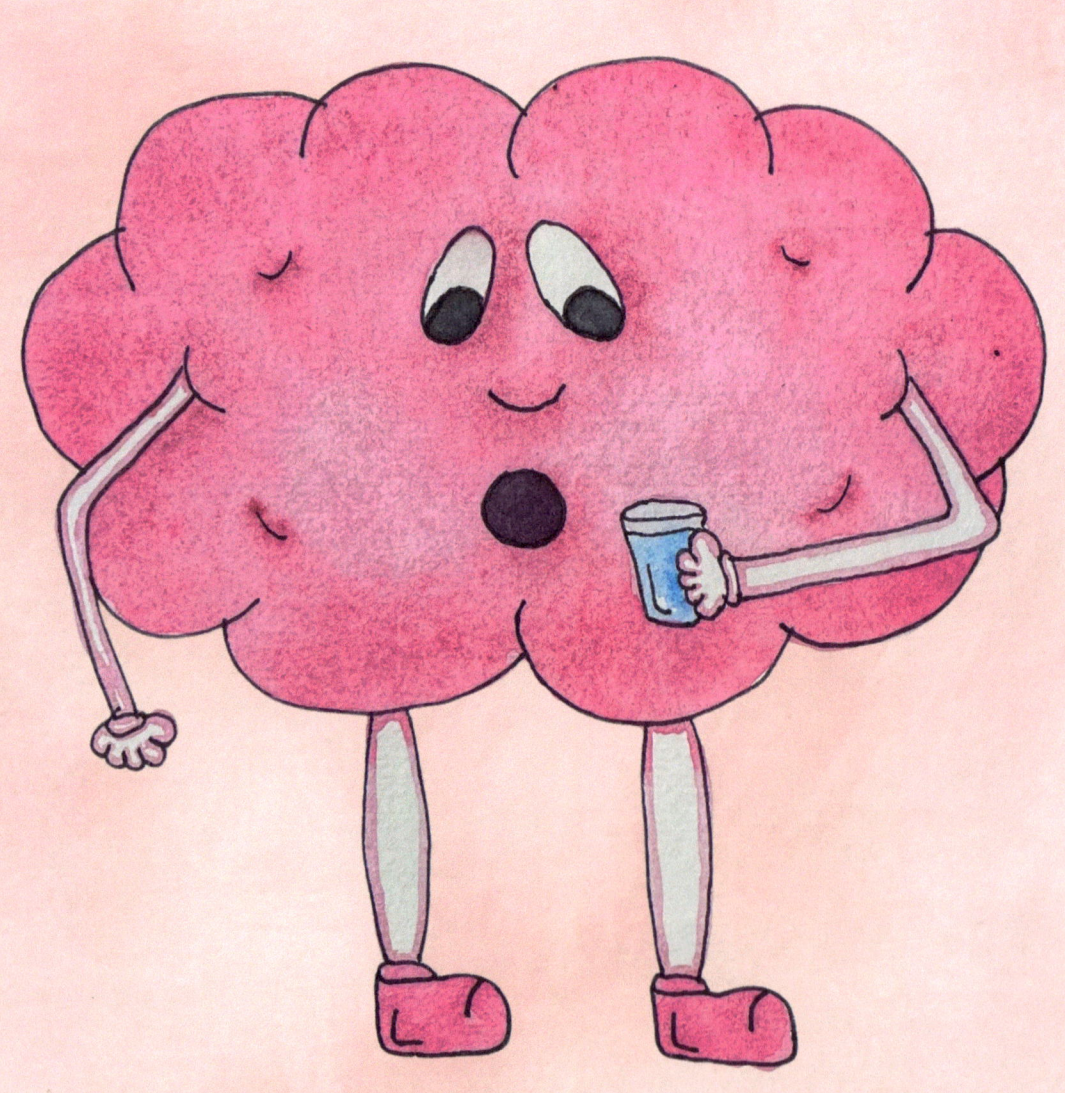

eating healthy food
and drinking water.

You can keep Buddy
the Brain safe by...

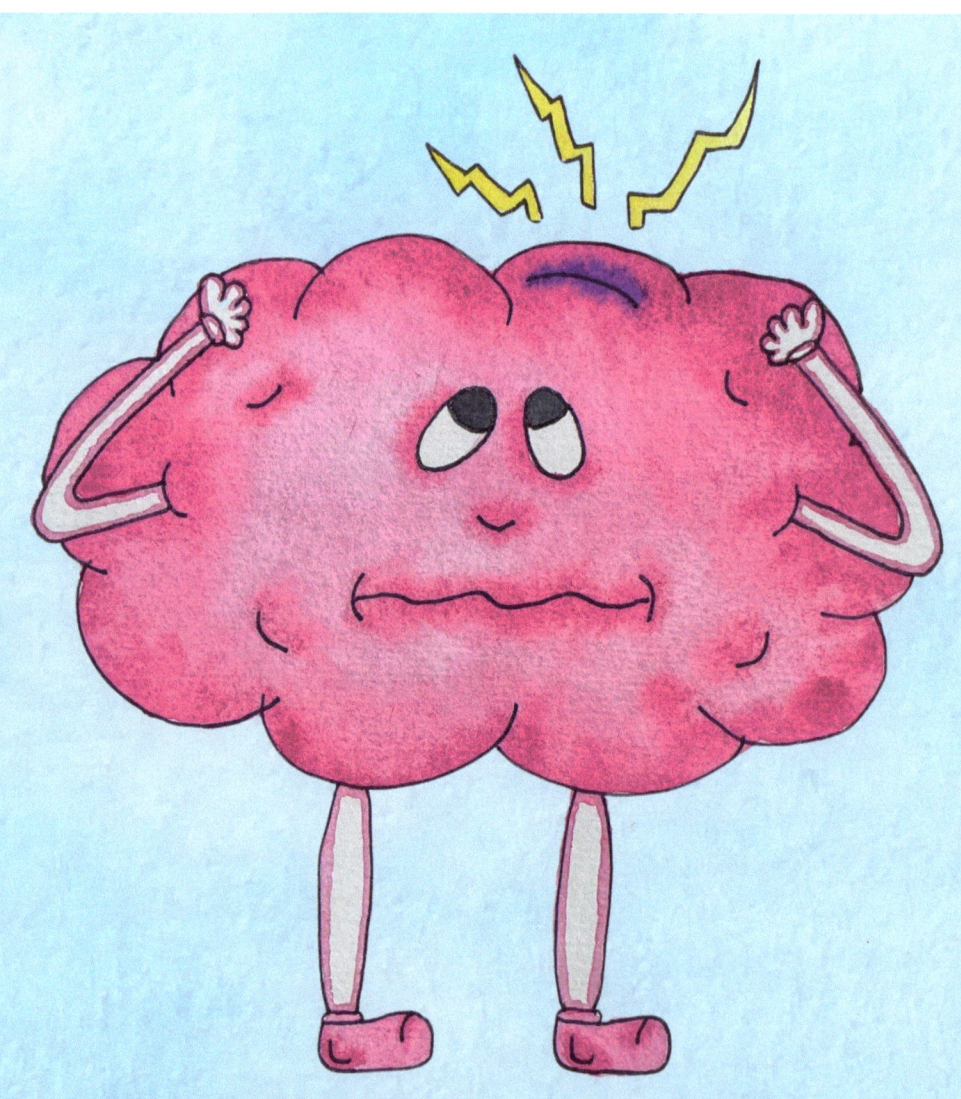

telling an adult if
you hit your head.

If Buddy the Brain gets hurt,

it is called a brain injury.

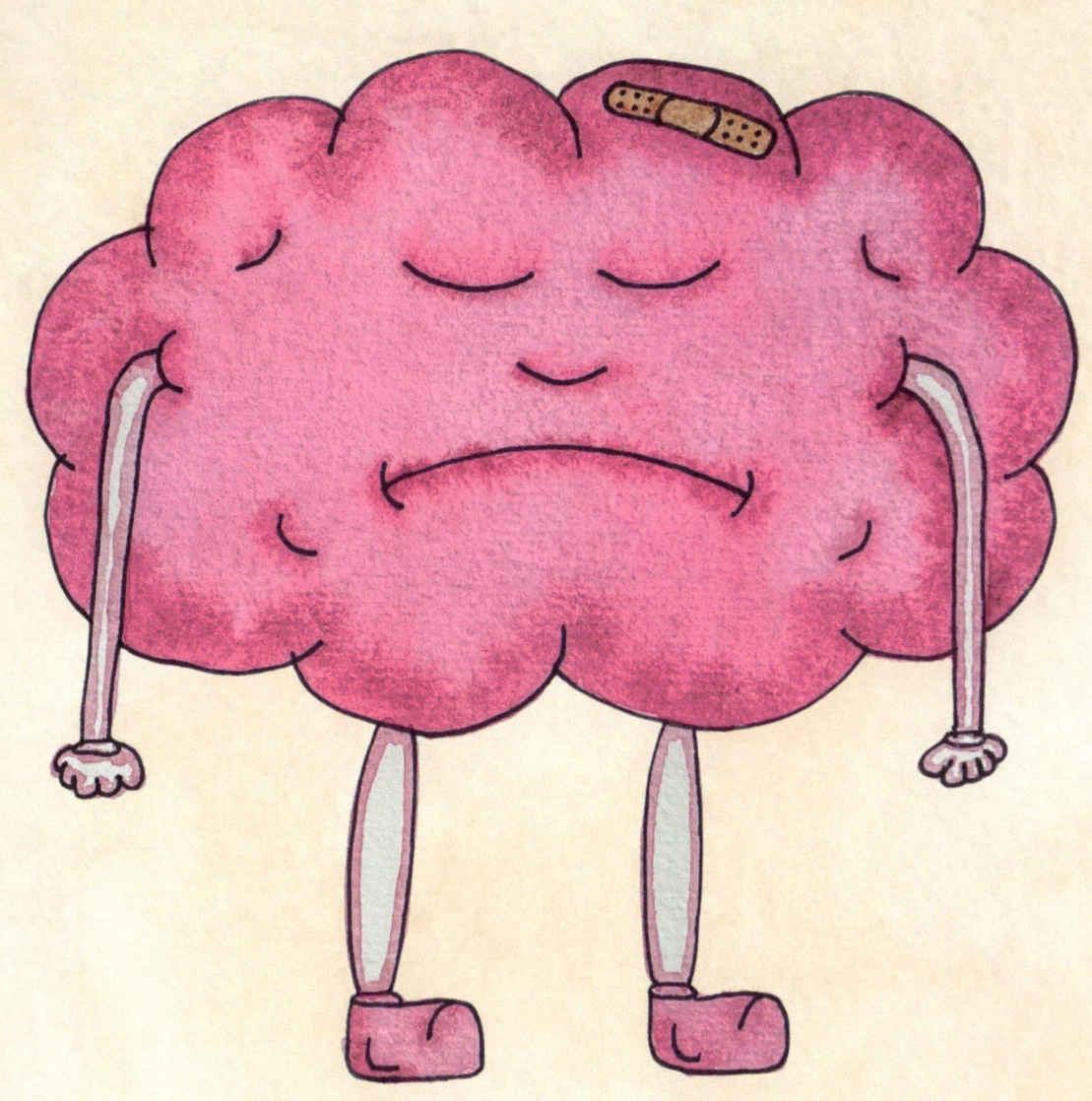

If you get a brain injury,

you may feel tired and
need to take a break.

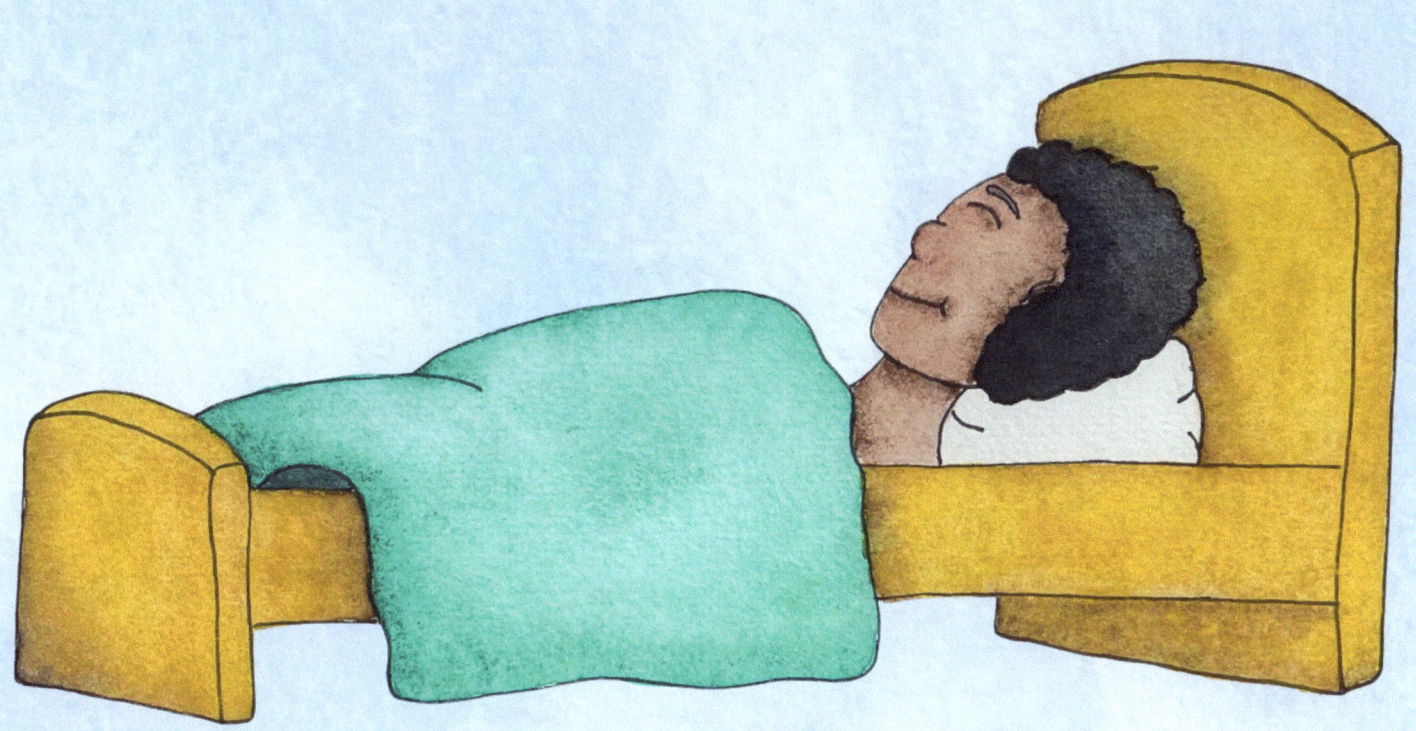

If you get a brain injury,

noises may feel
too loud to you.

If you get a brain injury,

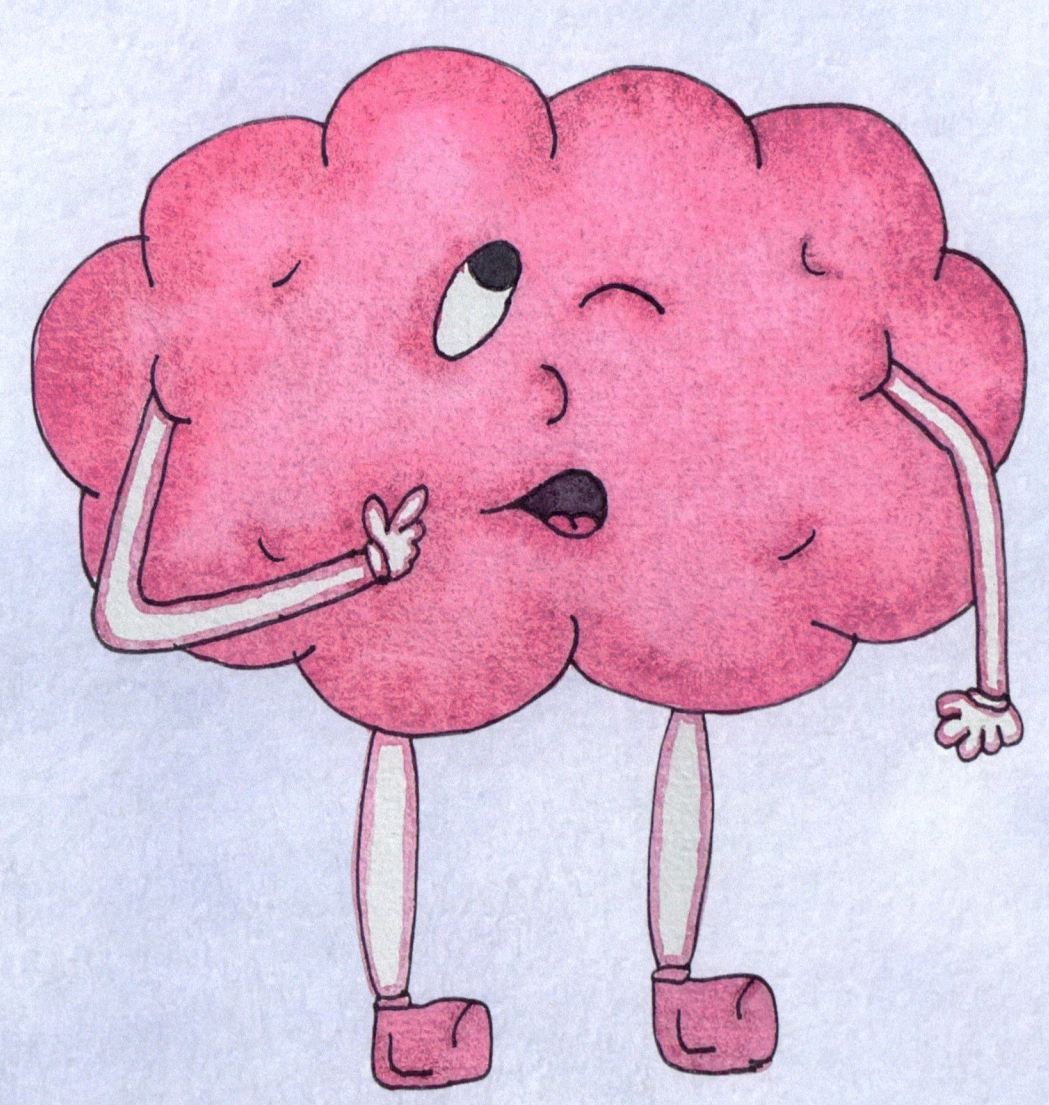

you may have a hard
time making choices.

Buddy the Brain is strong and smart.

He can get better and learn new things all the time!

Buddy the Brain loves you.

More fun and educational resources available at

https://alirheaume.com/buddythebrain

- Coloring Pages

- Learn how to draw Buddy the Brain

- Lesson Plans

Alison Rheaume has worked with children for years as an educator, with a Masters Degree in Health, Physical Education, and Recreation. Having sustained a brain injury herself, she understands the difficulty and importance of explaining it to children, so she developed Buddy the Brain. Ali is also a public speaker, artist, disability advocate, and accessibility specialist. Discover more at

https://alirheaume.com